Through a Grainy Landscape

Through a Grainy Landscape

poems by
Millicent Borges Accardi

POEMS COPYRIGHT © 2021 by Millicent Borges Accardi
COVER AND INTERIOR DESIGN by Alexandru Oprescu

All right reserved. Published by New Meridian, part of the non-profit organization New Meridian Arts, 2021.

No part of this publication may be reproduced, or stored in a retrieval system, or transmitted in any form or by any means, electronic, mechanical, photocopying, recording, or otherwise, without written perimission of the publisher, except in the case of brief quotations in reviews. For information regarding permission, write to newmeridianarts1@gmail.com.

LIBRARY OF CONGRESS CATALOGING-IN-PUBLICATION DATA
Through a Grainy Landscape
Authored by Millicent Borges Accardi

ISBN: 9781737249108
LCCN: 2021948412

CONTENTS

FOREWORD xi
INTRODUCTION xiii

A Man Sleeps, the Skies Move 1
With Eyes that Bear the Widowhood of Days 3
Because this One is Broken 4
The Most Vertical of Words 5
And Rage — a Pot of Orchids you Loved 7
Woman in a YelloX Dress 8
It was my Mother who Taught me to Fear 9
Of a Verbal Silence 11
Nothing Inside you but the Wool of your Sorrows 13
An Unsuitable Green 14
Carrying Someone You'd not Seen in 15 Years 16
I Abandon you Each Night 17
To you, who saw Fjords and Coral 18
I Smoke my Dead Cigarette in too Much Haste 20
Imposing its Rust on Everything 22
No Train will take us this Far 23
None of us Could Ever 25
Where your Mouth Delays the Cut 26
And There was Red Fish 27
The Architecture we were Born in 28
This Love is not Made of Blood 29
The Rocky Shore of this Water Clear 30
Letting Yourself Look Silly or Ridiculous 31
What Were you Doing in the Barn 33
The Fourth Ship 35
To the Same Place 36
So Much Needs to be Said 37
So you Believed in Fátima and Fadistas 39
You Swung Round on Yourself 40
You Swung Round 42

All Open to the Heat 43
With Myself I Disagree 45
You'll be Little More than This 46
The Graphics of Home 47
Mixing Drinks 49
Over Broken Bottles and Rivers 51
I Ask you not to Leave Tomorrow 52
Because You're Really Tired of it 54
Again, Between Past and Present 56
Scary Jobs 57
Counting Hammers at Sears 59
A Representation of Itself 60
Who or what is Being Born 61
Your Native Landscape 63
And We've Known This 65
When are you Going to Berlin 67
Sand Crumbling Down the Avenues in Porto 68
By Sea on all Sides 69
Shoes Visible in his Absence 70
Lacuna: A Blank Space or a Missing Part 71
Winter Arrives in Mourning, Unaccompanied 72
Drinkers of Silence, Emigrants from Other Worlds 74
This Necessary World of Objects 75
Far from the Honeyed-Wax Heart 76
More Nocturnal than the Sleep 78
The Only Answer to Silence 79
For Truth would be from a Line 80
Unmade 81
Still not Ilha Enough 82
And, at last, God Returns 83
I've Driven all Night through a Grainy Landscape 84

*Dedicated to
George Monteiro (1932–2019) and
Christopher Larkosh (1964–2020),
two of my literary heroes.*

> I've driven all night through a grainy landscape,
> on a motorway with dim and orangey lights
>
> —TIAGO ARAÚJO

> The light crossing the room between
> the two windows is always the same, although
> on one side it's west—where the sun is now—and on
> the other it's east—where the sun has already been.
>
> —NUNO JÚDICE

Many of the poems in *Through a Grainy Landscape* are inspired by lines from Portuguese and Portuguese-American poetry.

Foreword

In this book, Millicent has done something remarkable. She seamlessly alloys her poems with seminal lines from Portuguese and Portuguese-American poets, writing from their own culture and in their own native language. It is no small idea, no simple looking for a "hook" or a "trigger" for the poems she is about to write.

The writers she has chosen inform her thinking and her work. One of our central figures in Portuguese-American writing, Millicent has read and studied the poems of the Portuguese, both historical and contemporary. She has visited the homeland many times as a scholar and as a reader of her own work. Her many awards and accolades attest to her activity and commitment to her art and to the task of fostering greater understanding and appreciation of not only writers in America but also important writers in Portugal and the wider Luso-Phone world. This is a vital book for those of us whose heritage is Portuguese, but it's also an important book for American readers of every background and tradition. It stands as an esthetic bridge between cultures.

Through a Grainy Landscape is significant for all it does, but I must also say the formal body of this work—the sensual body of the poetry—satisfies that most important element in any art: beauty. There is beauty in the life that animates the poems, and the beauty of symmetry and surprise in their lines.

The book—as a whole—arcs through modulations of thought, observation, and reflection, and the placement of each piece is seemly so that the mind of the reader pleasantly does not rest, nor is it jarred. There is a music to the book's structure—not so much melodic as fugue-like, and strengthened with a steady build and careful ironies. And the poet graces us with wry looks into her fecund mind. A favorite of mine is the passage, My clothes were off the hangers. The books were being alphabetized into fiction as I talked in my head. I could go on with many snippets and samples, but you will find your own as you read and read in this wonderful book.

Millicent Borges Accardi has given us something that will live a long life and that will be read as one of the important books of the Portuguese Diaspora—and one of the important books of American poetry from the early years of our new century.

—FRANK X. GASPAR

author of *The Poems of Renata Ferreira*, *The Holyoke* and *Leaving Pico: a novel*

Introduction

Millicent Borges Accardi adds luster to her acclaim as a leading poet of the Portuguese-American experience with a new collection of breathtaking scope. She inhabits the new artistic frontier in exploring what heritage means to those descended from immigrants long established in the place of their dreams—"a dark mixture of all I have lost."

There's wariness about the past rolling itself up like carpets for storing in tandem with physical and spiritual unmooring as a contemporary fact of life. Even tattoos bleed and run, and shopping centers where memories were made vanish in Accardi's fusion of Luso/a saudade with her Californian sensibility. Revelations strike while shifting a car's gears. Break-up poems and paeans to silence contain the warning that there "…are no strata to strike matches on" because everything is uprooted, from history to the rules for marriage. A lemon-colored dress floats in like an oracular reminder that a young waitress with large dreams can easily turn into the lifer-waitress dishing up peach melbas for twenty years.

Most astonishing in *Through a Grainy Landscape* is the range, from the son of immigrants frightened of abandonment or the ancestor storing her Disneyland A tickets under her bed (note the defunct pricing system and the wry, sad fact that "A" rides were the least lustrous) to our current unrest in these Plague Years. Our times call for a resetting of sensibilities: while housebound, we can "look for kindness." If grief is "…shrapnel under the skin working a way out," and women are expected to be "zany volcanoes" before they explode into invisibility, it could be that whole new ways of being are set to emerge. I'll leave it to readers to discover how the poet frames this with an unforgettable image in the book's radiant conclusion.

—KATHERINE VAZ
author of *Saudade, Mariana, Fado & Other Stories*, and
Our Lady of the Artichokes and Other Portuguese-American Stories

A Man Sleeps, the Skies Move

from a line by Luis Quintais

It happens that way,
the sleep comes or not.
We stay awake and the worry
over a knock at the door,
at 5. When you are 5, your
parents sit you down and smoke.
They say. Ah. It is a difficult
thing. They say, you are our child,
born in America, and we are trying.
We filled out the paperwork.
We hired an attorney. There
was a problem with an entry
date. Our visa was late but,
we did everything we could.
There was a problem, you understand?
Columbia. That is what it is.
We moved and were a day late
in reporting our new address,
so we are trying. There is the sky.
We save money in a jar that looks
like water, the glass dense and broken,
in the jar. At any rate, you are born
in America. You are OK. Please, be
an adult. I know you are in kindergarten
and want to pick roses for your teacher,
but, please, listen and listen and listen
for a moment, listen for your whole life.

There may come a day when we might
be away. Memorize your Aunties number.
Take care. Watch the rain clouds. Do the dishes.
Do not fall asleep without worry.

With Eyes that Bear the Widowhood of Days

The ceiling of the ocean floor is fat,
with its tidal drop, a mere sandy slope, the
barrenness, now, a symbol, a lost meaning,
to catch, a rule that the Portuguese fisherwomen
on the shore above can attest to, easily
nodding in agreement that they are bound
together, like time they have wagered and lost,
a lifetime of fresh bets and new hands,
grown old with uncertainty, a rule,
a catch, a slip of the tongue and the
courtship will be over, lost to sea journeys far
away from solid-footed Terceira, where black glue
is the medicine of forgetting and a pause
is the known secret inside absence,
and where love is a shy attachment to hope, the
thaw that every woman, waiting here, tempts
with her own fate. On shore, they long to don sadness,
like a dark shawl around their forearms.
It is a uniform, encompassing wool, knitted
halfway between loss and joy.
The friendliest girls they used to be,
these women, now waiting on the land,
reveal happiness but with but a slight
mention or a holding note of the wind,
softly reminding them
of the men they used to love.

Because this One is Broken

There was a boat, there were many boats,
patterned after a fashion into a fleet.
There were Portuguese widows who prayed
and those who sang of sailors and their strong sea,
amid the sky that we wore like a cape.
There was a yellow radiance of sunset and how
it used to be. Please, ask me, husband, and I will bring
you a cup of Vinho Verde. It is what is done
when there are no answers. It is what we do
and what we have always done. There is a storm
gone blind against the curves of the land
we fall into. Tears over the bow of a ship
ashore, gone at sea for years. We wail and
throw our hands against the blanched wood
because that is what grief is, a primary feeling
that must be exposed. Glow, Storm. Blind.
Our men are an assault on we who wait
for them, as they travel to exotic lands,
deciding not to return to a way of life
that left them long before they unpacked
the dry bread in a cotton bag that we
sent along with them on their blessed journeys.

The Most Vertical of Words

The wake inside hides me.
It's like oppressive family histories
that shape and shame
and disgrace. Whether it happens
in childhood or later, the sting
of the blur of the bite
of the belt or the tongue,
the trace of it always
swells into an unmanageable
sorrow, a memory you cannot get
beyond. Many steel walls
go smooth, so you cannot grip
or hold or even hold onto
while others who should be held
accountable for, are not.
It is what it is and everyone says
that in jest and ill-perceived kindness.
Saudade, the universe has moved
on and given up its brightness
or fought through tremors
with deep fists of physical violence,
or words, but you are trapped
inside an identity you did not imagine
you would be. Outside
of the one area where you belonged,
where no one could question
your authenticity, beliefs and
no one would dare pull

the proverbial carpet out
from under your future. That is
What it feels like.

And Rage – a Pot of Orchids you Loved

from a line by Inês Fonseca Santos

Three years the tense flowers
have bloomed from the
green shoots, dormant
for months, now, the nerve curling
around inside a glass bowl as if
it were a beginner. I am
reflective and filthy, in this
house, looking inside the gaps
in the floorboards
for substance, as if this is how
life is supposed to be, a clean
floor, newly painted walls
every few years, the kitchen
scrubbed within an inch of
its life, as my mother used to say.
Spiders long gone.
We are past the newly-minted
version of marriage, all choices of
avenues we used to have
have become deserted. There are
no strata to strike matches on.
With a nod and a fixed stare,
you tell me it will always
be this way, and I fear
many times that you are right.

Woman in a YelloX Dress

Saved up from Pledge or Dove.
It was that way in those days.
Women-folk collected stamps
and coupons. You got a tank of gas
and received Corningware.
You hoarded grocery receipts
from Albertsons for red encyclopedias
and A tickets to Disneyland,
stored in a shoebox under the bed.
We had a den with deep shelves,
from bird's eye maple,
filled with starts and half-stops:
those multiple sets of volumes
from A to M, from A to D. Then the
stragglers of AB and AB.
On a whim, my mother saved up
for the yellow polyester sheath,
trim like the body of a bottle,
a treasure promised to her from soap
and furniture polish commercials,
the squeaky bright yellow pumps
that accompanied the lemon-colored
A-line drop dress, matched with
a heavenly scarf, that, when she wore
it, was as if she was every movie
star and every woman was vintage
Sophia-Loren-beautiful, on her way
to a Roman holiday in a topless
sports car, shrouded by her escape.

It was my Mother who Taught me to Fear

The irregular verbs of culture that brought
the family away from The Azores, to the promised
land of California, was, were been.
Shocking like a past to push away
And start over bore, born/borne.
As if invisibility could be
Run away from, a new start
in the garage of an uncle,
after a cross-country railroad
trip like pioneers, Los Angeles
was away from beat, and being beaten
down, the promised land was
to become became, begin,
a location that pushed away
and helped folks to start over,
pretending you were someone
else to fight, fought, fought.
To flee, fled. To approach
a way to make-over, redo, make-believe.
To start again. As if half-life
never happened. Not the Great
Depression of your grandmothers,
or the Great War, with its aircraft
carriers and new breed of
how to be and what to do. California
was a gifted promise for the melting
pot generation, goodbye to bend (bent, bent)
into shape. As the train car runs through
every state in the union, interwoven, interwoven

in a pattern called starting over,
in a safe place with a brand new method of
keeping, kept, kept. Where no one genuflected
on Sundays, kneel (knelt/kneeled, knelt/kneeled).
To recreate yourself from nothing is a wonderful thing.
Times were, you almost believed
it was possible.

Of a Verbal Silence

for Carlo Matos

Of a verbal silence,
We saw and thought
Riot, as if we could be not
Safe or sure but not still
Exactly otherwise or not
Not at all; it was on a lark
A spit or an urge that we set
Out to find a hawk, that bringer
Of change, a soul spirit animal
Who bears solidity
And a certain measure of trust
Into our lives that even embedded
In sadness we can have an old-found
Confidence of what we are doing
And the ashes are in the air
Blown like soft white seeds,
Milkweed, contained within
a shell that can travel
The wind, with bone fragments
and bits of earth, cloaking our fingertips
Like cotton gloves meant to
Protect. We say a few words,
Half-remembering what the last
Life of words should be, and we name
Off the flavor of our grief, all
Emotional and shaken, fingertips
Ashes, stone. We watch our souls

With a gentle kind of new urgency.
As they carry us to what must surely
come next: fingertips, ashes and stone.

Nothing Inside you but the Wool of your Sorrows

from a line by Frank Gaspar

The nothing inside you sits uncomfortably, like characters
in a book, dull components
with feelings—or erase that—not feelings
since they are last not first as the poet says,
they are vessels and sorrow is a weak definition
for what the sadness is that is going
on inside when you give up, not hope but
the capacity for an electrical joy, words
bearing individual meaning that you once took
to heart, in the heat of a moment, impossible to explain
but integrated inside the impossible, there is sorrow
and a sadness for the blanched allusion of nothing
thoughts you wished were as soft as wool.
As if you needed permission to liberate your own
limitations? To air them out. No that's not it
either. It is what it isn't unless you know worse.
Not everything they print in the newspapers
Is true. this navigating through a living worthy
of life, the keeping of an anxious soul even after the dense
body and blood are gone. What is it, parry to the universe,
that you say we remain only to travel into the next
cloth of happiness, the straight hem of the days
you spend wandering in place.

An Unsuitable Green

Shade of the color, the pattern
of clean fields, verde,
edible and charming, and, in
a way, happy. You see, the callow
nest of life is its newness and hope,
along with the promise of yet
what is meant to stay. Green is the lack
of winter, the end actually
of a short story. Green is
pleasantly alluring and easygoing.
There is kelly and torch song and
moss, emerald and sage.
What is most needed in the world,
perhaps, or what can take us
away from what we fear most
is green. People eat arugula to feel
healthy. There are apples,
fresh, new, tart and bitter. The burst
of a blast of verão
newness in your teeth
as you bite down the dense
skin is forever permanent.
The promises, there, are of
a particular happiness, the kind
most people don't want. Green is the
opposite of white or black. Drowned
in dense color, green is a sphere of false
brightness. There is newly-sawed

lumber, a sexy dress, cut
by a sexy track of old sweat
on a working body that is in its
prime and undeniable.

Carrying Someone You'd not Seen in 15 Years

The body goes light,   as if keeping   a piece of paper,
soft   and   awkward in your   arms.
There is a pulse   and so you   continue.
They   are without   words or sounds.
You imagine calling   a hospital   and screaming
into the phone at the ER nurse   to put   your mother
on the other end. It is night time, isn't it
always? And   you are in a hotel   in New York
City, two days   past Valentine's, and
one day   past the anniversary,   the first   year
your parents did not   dance   around the
room,   your mother   hovering   over your
father's shoes   as if she were   already.

I Abandon you Each Night

You abandon your waking
hours,
in soft squares, you try to neglect
your worries and shut down
the war-voices,   one on each shoulder:
and—if it is important
to you—you sigh awfully and listen,
or you ignore   and try   to avoid
the poison gas
because this is a solo   performance
that only you can sing despite the
urging of others   to couple and adore
and procreate. March. And—as if and as if—
It were a different protest.
Oh Man, I abandon   you each night.
   My heart ache,   my fears, my love,
my softness. It is as if I   roll over.
It as if I roll over   and touch nothing.

To you, who saw Fjords and Coral

title from a line by Renata Correia Botelho

The truth as you believe it
seems durable and unmoving,
like a parent's love, a parable
you believe in, can count on
solid like a hundred year
old wall or an established
company that you trust
will always be there, like
Montgomery Ward or
Sears. It is how it was meant
to be with no warnings or
caveats. It is the facts
and what is to be leaned on
when unsteady, a proverbial
storm in the port. The truth
As you learned it, sometimes
a lie or a word twisted just
to be nice, so no one's feelings
are hurt. I remember the first
time I tested the waters and
felt secure. The more I said it,
the truer it was, like practicing
scales on my flute or memorizing
lines for a one act. I sweated less
when I had time, and it was not
the night before the performance.
I remember when the world

ended that first time. It was me
and him, in an avocado green
kitchen and he had found something,
a secret he was laughing about
in a mean kind of way; it was as if all
history, all of my history, all of
the history of the world was over
in one phrase. He said the words
To me and I looked at him, clearly,
irises open, my skin heavy and plain.
I knew nothing would ever be
the same. It was a way out, a deviation
from a proposal. I said the phrase
and turned left at the ice berg
and lied. Completely, believably
and flawless. It was a shaky bridge.
and he understood.
My clothes were off the hangers.
The books were being alphabetized
into fiction, as I talked in my head.
My calves were tensed and ready to
lift up as I nodded yes,
and leapt off the cold edge of uncertainty,
ready to land into the nest—that was waiting
for me, hanging on a rope, far above my life.

I Smoke my Dead Cigarette in too Much Haste

from a poem by Inês Fonseca Santos

It was what I did in that time before,
when I knew I was 20 and I
could set apart my British Silk Cuts
into a single line, like dead soldiers,
match sticks, or wishes I failed.
It was my future composure,
my calm in the middle of a dense
place, where I could breathe in and
be happy, whether it was at a bus stop
or in the street. I could take a break
in traffic, giving a moment to think
of. Oh My. A red cabbage or loosies, and
then, I would smile and suck in the
smoke, a divine intervention
of sorts and, when I was out of sorts,
it would please me and calm me
and my terrors down and down would
come the person I was and even wily
new friends sympathized and
adapted to my sorts. I used to wrap my arm
around my back and hold my cigarette
in my right hand. It was what I was
when I was not there anymore. I smoke
my dead cigarette in too much
haste, with a rude urgency
that journeys away and determines that
hum, as if this is all the soul I will

ever have, after that, the man took and did
and threw me out until there is no more,
of a soul, and can still I see the dense red
ember, twisting and shelling and being alive,
all on its own.

Imposing its Rust on Everything

The rain gutters and the sharpness
of words, I fear their rust will eat away
at whatever was said or offered and so
it will always be that way and then
I will know it is but a whisper or a
spoken phrase that perhaps makes
all the difference. Today is Mother's Day,
and I wish for Audrey and her Jameson's,
the yellow polyester dress she wore in the photo
where I cut into an adult party
of ashtrays and celery, filled
with pimentos and cream cheese.
I think of choices I have made,
and that all of them were, at best, a 50-50
prospect shot. There is no ours unless
we are at play. No one person
can carry the load. And it was always
explained to me that the universe is like
a beach ball and when it drops
someone lets go.

No Train will take us this Far

There are 8 obscure words
for bodily harm
and so I collect immorality,
venturing for ribbons and pretty, in hope
for the last bastion of a local
penny store
while classmates, others,
saved Juicy Fruit.
My mother offered a short list of wear and tear
sundries to buy.
Still, I was drawn to the glass counter
near the sun, neck-high.
You could see the sidewalk
outside. The counter
with its basket of rainbow-colored rabbits'
feet. The translucent nails, some with
dried blood. For luck. Other nails shorn or chipped. More,
dangerously sharp. I wanted every
color. The canary yellow
that seeped into the fur, the gamey
odor they let off when I held them
in my scalding hands near my face,
a blue and a green. There
was a tan that I used to brush softly
so, against my cheek when I heard loud voices,
abuse, damage, disservice, I repeated.
Luck, yes, that is what I want.
Yes. I knew that was what it was,

shocking and comforting, and I wanted
a complete set, never comprehending
what I was getting
into, the sawed off feet , the strength,
sabotage, vandalism, violence, hurt—
all the things I wanted.

None of us Could Ever

for Michael Torres

It was a time
and oh what a time it was
the song goes when we felt
there was nothing that could be
done. Our days were a runaway
car we had to hold onto, no matter
what the speed or path way laid out
before us along the roar of the bright
noise not our own that we
we could not stomach when we
heard words like Go Home
or You Don't Belong Here.
We are a body and skin lock
to be locked up inside, our
very beings imprisoned
yet necessary. Like during
the Lisbon Inquisition
when it was common for Catholic
Priests to work with bruxas,
especially for banishments and cleansings,
healing those who had been bewitched.

Where your Mouth Delays the Cut

Make the energy arise from anger,
and breathe it out. While it is in the tooth
of the knife's cutting ridge that
takes a toll and makes it easier
to take in, there is a delay as if no one
is watching, a quick anger that
a child might devour, the singular heroic
power of innocence or naiveté
lit at attention by the thought
of independence. Anger, it is
what it hides, and you feel powerless,
to imagine otherwise. When the
knife cuts, the yielding vegetative
flesh changes form, causing a delay
and you'd pray to take it all back because,
because it is all that you've got.
Anger is the way your will demands,
a command you want to pass over
but cannot. It is sure and sweet and
urgent and prudent and it all
makes no sense, like the strong whiff
of cedar burning, blood that you catch
ahold of and run to.

And There was Red Fish

On the horizon that met with the quiver
of pining to make something different
that wasn't. It was a calling, a vocation
to run to the sea at midnight and curl
up into the cool sand, like soft snow
that felt like the wind of a fresh
time that had yet to be experienced,
saudade, a life yet unlived like communion
a beggar, a virgin. What you
longed for as a memory. Saudade.
Before it was lost, it was a dare
and an astonishment,
time to judge the mood and float
facing upwards among the salt
and the red fish muted in their
rusty stains all around the bodies
floating inside a cold window where
the moment was captured once
and caught and never would be
netted again—if ever anyone dared
stir or roll over and sink their
head back to shore where everything
and everyone was, there was a jackknife,
harsh and unbreakable. like a rat gone north.

The Architecture we were Born in

for Leticia Hernández-Linares

Portuguese was one of the seven deadly
jubilations, kept close at hand,
away from, the morcela made in hiding
as meu pai loaded the black blood
into the transparent casements we kept
inside the house, away from
neighbors. It was as if our lives
were on hold, encased in a prison
As if we were a secret not to be kept
but to be freed, no, as if we were
in hiding left from Terceira and New Bedford
wearing costumes called Long Beach
and Sears. And yes we were always here.
We told lies about the nowhere else
we had never visited, the islands
we backed away from. Dropped into
the East Side of where we landed,
in a proper tract California Bungalow
the third owners in a short line of lives
lived. The doctor with a ginger cat who used
the front entry as his waiting room.
We were in disguise, afraid of the
serenity we might never feel, the horror
of telling the truth. Existing in a variety
of lost stages of fitting in and awkward
strength. We knew vices, deception
and the way our imaginations were
helpless to fight against the
anonymity of what is called America

This Love is not Made of Blood

Floating briefly around my
heart, inside the caption above
my cartoon head. It is what walks
inside me and calls me by name.
This love is not solid matter,
or fleeting. It is a power I can
call upon when I am feeling
weakened by large things
like life and all that encompasses
it. The doom is a mirrored puzzlement
that sits beside me on the city bus,
a distraction when I hear
the noise of threadbare brakes and
my street called out, Junípero,
muffled by an overcoat and footsteps
climbing metal stairs,
with their grooved teeth, a sight
I can barely see from my bench
seat at the back of the bus,
where I hide behind a copy
of Little Women, its library
spine, broken down and torn, the
yellowed checkout card stamped
with a purple date two weeks away.

The Rocky Shore of this Water Clear

written on a theme by Lucia Eugenia Orellana Damacela

Red Gram peas laid out on the typewriter table, like small apples as his wife sorts thru a mountain. The man from New Bedford waits in a track suit as muddled as his Portuguese accent, muttering shh shh, his shoulders bent up toward his dark head as he fumbles with a portable radio on the pull-down ironing board next to him and the Press Telegram Saturday crossword at his hands, where he fills in words he knows like desk, pencil, and garlic. Worn, under the table, his brown sandals wide and flat with scratched leather and buckles the size of fists, remind him of resiliency, brittle like a crucifix inside a swear word, the crudeness put aside for a moment of American Wheaties in a bowl of reason served cold. This humility that he has shoved down with a spoon is a place he does not have the courage for.

Letting Yourself Look Silly or Ridiculous

He said that was it, and the refrigerator
was his. Leaving a note in his schedule book,
the color of ripe plums, "break up with M"
Implying I was tightly wound, with goals
and lists and friendly parents who wanted us
to get married so they could chip in
for a condo. After all, it was the suburbs
and could have been the 50's or 60's or any generation
of an era except now, with the ugly tears,
and notes scribbled about a Berkeley
weekend to blow off the grief with clams
casino at Castagnola's on the pier.
He said he could not afford to move
out, and neither one of us were ridiculous
or silly enough to think outside the box springs
of our jointly-rented apartment, so we unfixed
this shit and stopped speaking to each other,
ditching in at 2am cause that is what 18
year olds do when they are breaking
up their new bodies into separate pieces
for the first time. They share a single bed,
too naive to consider the floor, or even
a neighbor's pull-out. It was how
it was in those haze-of-a-lifetime-long-
ago-drunk-and-high days, when earnings
were counted in coins on the floor,
stacked up into paper cylinder cones
and taken to the clinic on Monday.

It was a scramble race for cash,
and hours amid a water way of bad restaurant
jobs with bad bosses who wanted everyone
to work off the clock and demanding waitresses
meet them in the walk-in freezer for
hits off the Redi-whip and a grope.
It was a time of trust and sex as if this age
would always be like a small new life frozen
inside as if we would always, always
care this much about everything.

What Were you Doing in the Barn

They said, maybe you were deep sadness,
that you could help dig deep, the harm
and vulnerability made worse since.
There are no more barns in the city and ages
old barber shops and family grocers
have been taken over by big money,
with hipsters who want to tell it like it is,
only sarcastically. In Lincoln Heights
alone, there are families, renting 50 years,
displaced when the Starbucks
moved in and rent soared to $3,000 a month.
A woman in her 90's, still sits on a porch
where she raised her children, walking
to the coffee shop every day, looking
for a pet dog she last saw twenty years ago.
There is a lawn chair and newspapers. Hope
that some new-found kindness was kept
inside women's work.
And that a sickness that rings hollow as
soon as you head back on your way
to Mount Washington.
It is a long way home, the novelist
said and no one can go back. But,
then there is the roof and loft and the
grain elevator, which has not been inspected
in this new century. That comes to mind.
There is time and time again, a movie-fantasy
where there is a living room, with its

stage coach lamp and the all-lit parlor
is covered in plastic and mother comes
out with a pitcher of cream, thru those holy days
of the summer when the sidewalks are
rolled up before the city lights come on.

The Fourth Ship

for Carmen Tafolla

Had no name, we never spoke of the passage
from Terceira to New Bedford,
nor of the war he fought in Europe
and Turkey, what was then Anatolia,
a land of celestial blue, returning home
back from the sea with a thick woolen sailor's
uniform that smelled like cedar and straw,
and a box of swords. His friend
Bud had a tattoo where the ink had run
into the skin so the former image was
no longer visible, more like a large
blocked out forearm of green-blue
colors, like a long sea, like a country,
joined to water, with no housing
to be found or excitement either.
There was a confidence over the dinners when
Bud traveled from Alaska to California,
for a brief meal of clams and sopas.
We gathered as if it were an occasion
like we were treading water around
submerged bombs. He said he was
tooling turquoise and silver, shaping it soft
by hand over time, gifting me with a ring
in the shape of a turtle with a turquoise
stone for the rounded shell, and a tail
in the shape of the letter "U" that pinched
the skin around my finger when I wore it.

To the Same Place

It was hey and let's stop,
and pause for a moment because
I want a few words
with you for a moment.
Let's stop under the arbor,
here, where there used to
be greenery and horses,
with the owners before the last
before them, when I was a
kid. The horses used to snip
up to the fence and brush
their noses through the gaps
in the sky, looking through
me as if I were either nothing
or a strong catalyst for
their freedom. Hey, I took out
the trash today, three days
before I was supposed to.
I hunt for the small happiness
in chores these days. What is
inside the dome of being housebound
is to look for kindness, for
truth. To plow ahead even very
small victories, celebrated
enormously, have power. As if you are
a child attempting
to affix a small child-proof cap
back on a plastic bottle
and keep failing.

So Much Needs to be Said

So much needs to be
said. There is thickness
and the air feels dark
as if the world
is delayed on a corner near
by to catch the bad
news, starting with? They had two
good seasons where the leaves
were dry and our dreams owned
special powers then, it was easy.
Not fast. The creek was rushing
full, reminding her of an old
soldier, spitting into a
tin case, with red and black
polish sitting in his hand flat,
like a pack of easy cigarettes.
I'll bet he has a carton of those
too. On the carpet next
to his dresser is a shoe rack
and he stands, there, where
he puts on his tie every morning,
standing on one foot as he eases
on slip on loafers and pulls through
a double-Windsor knot, wrapping
the left hand around twice before
sorting it through. He hears
sirens and looks out the low window
to the backyard, already heating
up with smoke, like Easter fog

coming in. He folds a daily
white handkerchief for
his side pants pocket,
and checks the gold watch
he kept through Ellis Island
before smoothing the surface
of his 1928 liberty lady half-dollar for luck.

So you Believed in Fátima and Fadistas

from a line by PaulA Neves

Like someone who wanted
to hide, you believed in the past,
a statue of Fatima, in milky
blue, looking like a soap bar.
The dawdling words hidden
in your pocket, like warmth
on a cold day. To wish for
sandals you dreamed of days
when you did not have to bury
yourself under the bed,
Or wear pants under your skirt,
You hummed the slow fado
music under your breath
and considered a time where
walking home was not a test
in fixing life. On a table near
the kitchen was an unfinished
model of the Queen Mary
with its shiny smokestacks, glued
black, carelessly with Elmer's glue.
The sable brush in your hand,
a child in exile, the sea a distant
eight blocks away.

You Swung Round on Yourself

And spit into the drawer,
in the built-in bureau,
containing the family
photos of Terceira. The
old country. Those days
of Art singing with a swing
band, when he still smoked
cigarettes and wore
a white dinner jacket
with tight lapels just
like Sinatra, the skinny
legs in black, creased pants
with the wool crinkled
at the ankles. There was
a fire. You pretend it cost
you everything, the crib
In the attic, the paintings
of rodeos in Santa Rosa,
riders leaning backwards
etched out in red pastels,
You see the hobnail
glass shoes, sealed
in a cabinet with a lock
and the long shelf of vinyl
records, ear-marked
for you, a mother's blue violet
china, with the odds
and ends of three

generations of lifetimes
spent in a bungalow on a street
named for a red fruit,
a house bought in the
1950's for 12 thousand
dollars, from the original
owner who left black
and white photos of a family
sledding in the snow in
the mountains that you
discovered on a treasure hunt
as a child and always
always remembered.
The builder said he had sat on
a keg of nails watching
workers hammer in
the bird's eye maple door
frames and the grooved
wooden floors you roller-skated
into dust.

You Swung Round

In a direful way, reaching forth
In a wave of wanting, like a woman
Is supposed to want babies and a home
And a man, to want to attract anything
And anyone better than her as a lifetime
Of being a mere child, a poor thing, a lesser
Than to be silenced and chit-chitted away
To a moon launch of pillows on a bed
Somewhere in a shared cell of misery,
Is the female of the species only a vision
To want
To attract, a steadfast of do or don't
A lifetime based on one I do?
A have and a have-not no matter what?
The only gender to instantly transform
In three phases only: child, mother, invisible.
Are women meant to be zany volcanoes
That explode upon command until they
Are invisible? The crate, the bath, the vast
Picture of auspicious dexterity known
To man only as the next best thing.

All Open to the Heat

We found them
in the summer patio that
we called "The Lee,"
with its green corrugated
roof, and windows on three sides,
with bamboo shades.
I could have lived there for
an epoch, crawling
over the painted window sill
to get to the bathroom
where there was a blue
toilet and vanity made of seashells.
It was luck and love
and hot stone heat
we found there, when
the floor retained its
warmth, long into evening,
when our bare feet crossed it,
it was like fire walking.
In bed, we tucked in, under our
ambitions. Forthright liars
we were, all of us, grabbing onto
lines we had heard at adult
parties in New Bedford
as if they were Sunday-speak.
It was real pell mell
and hurry down, only to slow
the pace of the hours. When our reddish

faces and burnt backs ached,
we slathered on syrupy balm,
with the odor of coffee.
Our hearts made up with red
lipstick. We all longed to marry
a mollusk, if we could, his briny star
insides clinging to the rocks in earnest.

With Myself I Disagree

In the collars of the corners,
their starchiness upholds
a portrait of how things
should be played out,
or executed. The collars
hold up tight against the neck,
as if they are holding back
a country, bad for immigrants
and children. Bad for everyone
except those who harvest perceptions
of the past, or, as they think,
they are more elegant and favoring
a particular world
view that is upside up,
behind the back of those with gnarled
knuckles gripping on tightly,
as if this generation means
all of it. To everyone. Yes.
They mean every word.

You'll be Little More than This

Someday, as if it were a miracle.
So low. The time is never-ending
and yet. But. This is the moment
you dreamed of. And then you didn't.
It changed, and you stopped being
across the road, divided by a city,
you stopped being sad for birthdays
and holidays, those
random dinners out, to celebrate
a new job for example. You remember
a time when you used to buy silver
hoop earrings and leather pumps,
a velvet backless dress
that had a pocket at the hip.
Disappointment, you swore it
would not happen and, yet, it did
any way. You became the great
Aunt you made fun of, who
took out her false teeth at dinner,
who made you cry when you had
leg braces. The woman who was hit
in the head with a hammer by her first
husband, and, yet, before that? Your
grandfather said, no one could laugh
like Anna did.

The Graphics of Home

Were broken by the Great
Depression, the textile mills,
and the golf ball factories.
We came from The Azores
and the mainland and Canada,
settling in Hawaii and New Bedford
and San Pedro, the original
Navigators. No one was documented.
Here was what I learned at home
thru the lifecycle of a shirt.
Polyester and cotton, it arrived
in the mail, from Sears,
sent as a hand-me-down
from Fall River, carefully washed
and ironed and pressed,
in a tomato box that had been
repurposed and wrapped in brown
paper and smelling of stale
cigarettes. That shirt was worn
and washed and used many times,
as if it had been new. When they
frayed, the elbows were mended,
and torn pockets were reconnected
with thick carpet-makers' thread.
When the sleeves were too worn
to restore, they were scissored
off to make short sleeves and then
the new ends were folded and hemmed

until no more and then there was the time
when the sleeves were cut off
entirely, to create a summer top
or costume for play time, sleeveless,
perhaps a vest for a pirate.
When outgrown and too worn
for even that, the placket of buttons was removed,
in one straight hard cut along the body
of the shirt front, through and through.
The buttons were pulled off by hand,
for storage in an old cookie tin,
the cloth cut into small usable pieces
for mending, for doll clothes, for
whatever was left over. The rest, torn
into jagged rags for cleaning and, if the fabric was soft,
used for Saturday's dusting of the good furniture
in the den. Whatever was left, was sold
by the pound, wrapped and rolled into
giant cloth balls, sold to the rag man
who made his rounds in the neighborhood
all oily and urgent and smiling as if
his soul were a miracle of naturalized
birth.

Mixing Drinks

There was the lemon
polyester dress,
matching shoes and the
purse gotten for free from
a soap company after
box tops were collected.
This was the year my mom's
hair was bright red, and I helped
mix drinks for home parties,
the limes placed carefully in
a circle on a plate, the salt
and peanuts next to Brew 102
beer. There were jars with green
olives and chewy candy cherries,
the make-shift bar on top of the
New portable dishwasher at the edge
of the kitchen, not quite fitting in
the storage porch. The guests
arrived while I was in my robe
and fussy slippers, I had a runny
nose, and was querulously handy with
a dull knife, slathering pimento
spread onto celery and battling
the urge to scoop out the black
olives from the spiral-mouthed jar
of Lindsey's. My dad heated up
linguisa sausage and put on the
music, ranging from Peggy Lee

And Sinatra to Fado. The doorbell
rang and people were shuttled
inside, gathering near the fireplace
where the ashtrays were. The shots
and the aguardiente were hours away,
long after I was sent to bed, with strict
orders not to shake or stir.

Over Broken Bottles and Rivers

We sailed, unequaled amid
a stupid sea of hard knocks.
You were no sharp match
for me, a somber artifact,
housebound for years, hidden
inside the world as I used to
know it would be. There were
once important times, when we
traveled, and then there
was wool. I touch your neck
like a weak signal, poor and too
ordinary to care anymore.
I am exactly what people think
of me, a dark mixture
of all I have lost. There is no one
to attract or bring home to me anymore.
The heavens, they are but a bright
whiff of distraction above, mere
remnants of the truth which is
just about to be voiced.

I Ask you not to Leave Tomorrow

In my own sort of pulling
needy way that I have when
I try to sort
myself out of a bad place
I ask again in
my fictional conversation,
interrupting the words
upon the page of
the one I walked in on
in the middle of a book,

when I feel the pull of tears
at the back of my throat
as if I am going to strangle
myself,

I am static and stable,
a woman aboard a slow
boat to China, the song
my dead
parents danced to at
their wedding at the
Seafarer's Chapel
when they were young
and on break, from jobs
at the new Sears
on Acushnet Ave,

already on their way
home for malasadas
moving rapidly
to a wad of 50 years
of a marriage
lived cross-country
mentally, inside a story
only I know now,
during the far away past time
of what was never meant
to be.

I fear the new promised hint
of a place now tugging
where everyone
succeeds in their weeping,
and I look for signs that
this is true.

Because You're Really Tired of it

And everyone asks how you are
and cautions you to make sure to take
care of yourself. Because you're really
tired of it, the arrhythmia and the transplant
tests and the endless years of waiting even
after you thought it would come about
in six months or a year. It turned into
a sight of slight and illness and no one
understands about the fact that it will
get worse before it gets better and all that,
If it is not enough of a problem already
and you know the breath comes more
slowly, and it's a task to get up from the couch
and even simple tasks are slowly and suddenly
difficult. It is as if the soil has dried up
and there is no room for you to root.
Everyone says get well soon and seems
disappointed when you don't or can't
and whatever and whatever, and it does
not matter anymore since the universe
of friends and neighbors you used to have
and count on have shifted as if in a slip
fault earthquake or back alignment that
went bad. You want things just to just to,
just to—maybe, perhaps, be normal for
now or for later and nothing seems to stick.
It's topsy-turvy where black is white
and the messy world is grey, all grey

and messy and there are weeks when
no one seems to care about the lost
wishes you used to mumble about,
about when you
could not see the sun for a whole year,
and you missed the sun every day and
missed the eclipse too. I'd like to see
the sun again. Hurry back. I'd like to
drink some rosé too. All around I walk
with my eyes closed, as if I can find my way.

Again, Between Past and Present

Ago, when she wore green clogs
and a minho dress with a
clasp at the back.

There was yellow and there were
sunflowers, packed into a fresh
vase, with its over-flowing of
murky water.

Time is not what it seems.
She considers childhood when it took
centuries for the second hand
to make it around the circle.

And 30 years ago, she knew what
dress everyone wore, with the lace;
it was maybe a few days

ago when she wore green clogs
and a minho dress with a
metal clasp at the back of the small
of her waist. When it all ended.

Scary Jobs

Were quick and slow like the Fox
Trot and the work slipped through
our hands like soft olive oil.
When we went down for the count
and held our breath. It was a live
play where we acted out college poverty,
working beside minimum wagers
who had rent and families, undocumented
workers for whom an extra dollar
meant nowhere or golden.
Not considering that her pack
made wolf-born money spent
on a prom dress or pot or a pair
of tennis shoes She had to have every
moment until she didn't,
And the world needed her to
participate in this acting play,
this down time as a way to get turned
in the direction of being wane
and sane and sober, like someone
visiting a prison who trips on a mop
and lands in a cell for the next
35 years. It was not always this
way. Scary work used to be fun
like sticking your feet into a pool
off-season, or licking off the spoon
when a cake is mixed. She was not sure
when things changed but they surely

did. It was, perhaps, the first time
the heat was turned off, or when
her ten year old car stopped running
and could not be fixed for under $1,800.
But, maybe, it was a realization
that no one is making fun of
that waitress anymore, who is putting together
a peach melba for the past 20 years,
while she funds twin daughters thru UCLA.
She's not off on a spree, celebrating
Xmas in July with bottle born
champagne and wiping off the sauce from
a spill on her apron and smiling at the manager,
knowing it won't be bad cause none of this
is real. Not the bus rides or the
laundromat or blow jobs for the landlord.
It will end like every movie and the Klieg lights will
shine and come up slowly when the credits
roll and the back doors will open to early sunlight,
on a spring semester cause this is the middle
of the afternoon and no one is surely or certainly
or everly scared after all, right? Alright.

Counting Hammers at Sears

She started babysitting in 6th grade,
and then she sold tickets at winter baseball
and took inventory at Sears
(counting hammers and screwdrivers).
She worked at a fish restaurant
as a smiley hostess, working at three sign shops
(constructing signs and vinyl letters)
thru her first year of community college.
Then, multiple waitress jobs
(at Queen Mary, Jolly Rogers, Parker's Lighthouse).
She put in a few years as an artist model
at maybe 30 different art schools.
From there, she segued into grad school,
teaching assistant, ESL tutor.
Then, it was adjuncting and work on the line
at a dog food manufacturing plant.
She sees a little bit of herself in every place
she goes: restaurants, oil refineries, hotels.
No matter what she wears, customers
find her in the aisle or near the side-work
station and ask for extra ice or "where
is the dry wall?" People yell, Miss or You
or even Over here when they see her turn
their way, as if she were always on duty.
Once, celebrating Thanksgiving
in San Diego, she remembers being on her way
to the bathroom, when a lady at another table
handed her a plate with a half-bitten toast
and said, "more Sanka, please."

A Representation of Itself

And the world is my idea,
except when it isn't,
and Schopenhauer will
solve all the problems.
When we dance this
close or when the solutions
elude us, as parents tuck
us in late at night after dancing
and high ball Harvey Wallbangers,
smelling of boozy wickedness.
It was a rare existence,
this being left along
to fend on one's own,
long after it was well enough,
and so, it was life or sadness
or a lack of ambition that
caused the downfall, to take
away whatever it was that
We thought-imagined
In our dreams as navigators of the seas. For a moment
It was truly, really, hold on
tight, belonging
to us. Once and for always.

Who or what is Being Born

It's a matter
of moving forward
my husband likes to say
If you throw shit
off a ship and it floats backward,
you are moving ahead.
If it sinks or moves forward,
then you are in trouble.
A year when there is April
Fools and Easter on the same
day would seem fraught
with errors of opportunity
for rebirth as well as mirth,
as well as a few surprises,
like that one time when I poured
vinegar into a snifter
and served it as brandy
or when someone with tight
lips handed me a thick
glass of water to take
with my aspirin and it turned
out to be vodka, which
would normally have been
nice but not at 9am when
I was home sick with a cold
on April Fool's day and vodka
was the last thing I imagined
besides the fever and the box

of tissues on my bedside table.
It was first, a willingness of wanting
to be healed not poisoned.

Your Native Landscape

Lies, it does not begin
to describe the terrain
of grief, not like a sadness,
not like a leg amputated,
not like the world is a different
place, not like a horse that is shot
or a dog you have to put down.
Well-meaning people say
"Life goes on" or "Take your mind off things"
They say, move along, go for a walk,
Try yoga or throw yourself
into work or a new project.
All creatures are meant to face
this loss of a parent, why can't
we all just get old together and age
as kinfolk, bundled in heritage
sharing down to earth wisdom,
like a line in the front
of the family Bible that everyone
signs and dates, carefully, with a line
at the end of the date that never gets
filled in. Oh, and if that it were true?
Even if there was peace at the end
or if death came suddenly
then, all at once. Even if, the explosion
of emotion lasts, long past usefulness,
like land mines in South East Asia,
going off when crops are gathered or the dirt

is raked through for new seeds.
Bang, it happens. Even years later
back in America, you run past Clifton's
or see the Dupar's sign and the past
slams into the present, in new ways
that the future has yet to consider
or digest. Grief is like that,
it's shrapnel under the skin working
a way out. A person born
in a specified place, aligned with a land
made whole because of birth,
whether subsequently existing there or not.

And We've Known This

based on a line by Lin-Manuel Miranda:
We know history will remember this tragedy, and its tragedians.

As sure as it is when time
ends and you are in Dutch,
as in, you have me over a barrel
of the old harms and imposters,
rearing their disordered
heads, the guilty displayed
freshly on a table like
uncut meat, finished and ready
for the knife. Then the mouth,
a contraction of what is,
as if these women had peeled
their own lives away from their skin.
We pretend we are on a holiday,
when the children are taken,
when the borders are closed,
when it is considered free and easy
for others to play loose with new lies.
Hell, we never saw this coming,
but it has been here all along,
a closed deficiency of character,
like a man with no moral compass.
This is what we have, instead
of living. So, we cut, we use, we rise
above the global unity
until we are too old to impound
or imprison. There is an exchange of

a want for a want. No needs
met—just a weak understanding
that one side does not have
the only right of passage. We cut,
we use, we impound. Thick
with kindness, we are full
of tragedy and a need for love,
suppressing all the world before us,
to just be understood.

When are you Going to Berlin

There was a train from Prague
in the middle of the night with old-timey
red velvet rooms in first class.
The conductors came around
when we were in a tunnel and
took everyone's passports
in the darkness, as if it were the cold
war or the Big War, no one spoke
English or pretended not to.
The towns shifted by in slow,
non-urgency where Dresden was bombed
out and another city ornate and intact,
all lost eventually to transit speed
and a lack of sun, I would have
imagined there were bridges
and trollies, carrying children laughing,
but the windows were thick and cold
to the touch, it could have been 100
nights as we roared slowly but surely
through the night of tunnels and
sordidness. There were metal sounds
and the cars rubbed against each other,
with gaps of dark air and a hay ground
below when the train car connections pull
apart roughly, as if they would split
open like a grapefruit, into segments
of fruit and skin.

Sand Crumbling Down the Avenues in Porto

for Amy Sayre Baptista

The temper of the ocean buzzes
Through the downward avenues
Leading to the shore, the fish-wives,
As they scrape with a file, the Dourada
Into sidewalk gutters, in front of soaked
Boxes topped with salt and dirty ice.

Earning their keep in words and insults
They bear down with their teeth
As they throw each fish onto a mountain
Of more fish, calculating how many
Crates they go through.

Back stiff and fearing solitude,
Like the decaying mansions up on
The street of good friends, near
The old jardim district, with its
Broken iron gates and tumbled
Front yards.

The world is a vein to open and let
Leave be, in a rush of a wave,
Living is only for the direful,
Those who choose to be the river,
Narrow and sweeping as it
Meets with the mother Atlantic
And joins, next, better, always,
How easily it is choked back into
The larger body as it gives up.

By Sea on all Sides

from a line by Inês Fonseca Santos

An island, a loss of time
in Pico. Like, hey, like every day stood
in as a substitute for a week or ten years.
And, after a certain amount
of time, it does not matter
who is the president, what day
it is, the lies asked of my mother
to decide if she could live
on her own, in a dwelling of her
choice. How much is 2 plus 2
And, if it is wrong then what she said
was true. Do I stop taking buses
and walking to the Dollar Store?
Is it out of sorts for time spent solely trying
to be a good Catholic person, and who
are you to tell me otherwise, to gladly
decide if my reply of Nixon or Kennedy
is correct, in this moment when you are
asking and saying and confusing me.
Repeating that I must be a part of Yes,
and I do want to plant tomatoes in the yard
with artichokes and have family gathered
around the picnic table on the porch that Papa
had made. You have no idea as to what was
going on during the last century when
women got the vote and the earth spun
a little slower on its axis and no
one said it mattered anyway whether it
mattered about Monday or Friday.

Shoes Visible in his Absence

Hide around the anger, hidden
As if they were the corner of a house
Unobtrusive and ordinary
Dead in a way without a human
Giving them life, setting them apace
Marching down the hallway
With a mild cough, ever-present
The back and forth of loss, like someone
Painting a wall, deliberate and uncaring
Only wanting to find the ending to this
Heaviness that has been cast upon
Him. The shoes bear the burden
Of their owner, worn inside, bruised
On the heel and the long brushes
Of pressure inside the painted toe where
Too tight laces have worn there
And beaten down a quick walk
That was once hopeful for the future.
Instead, there is grief, generosity and faith
But hidden there, inside the cloth
Of a time spent hiding and running
Away, into the arms of those more
Generous and kinder. Those who could
Never change him, even though
They thought they could.

Lacuna: A Blank Space or a Missing Part

The invalidity of faith,
A state of nostalgic longing for
Or securing of a profound melancholy
For an absent tongue, an absent island
Where we were born and left and then
Never born to, a family abandoning its
Land and itself moving into a larger state
Of being Memory alone, a loss of the image
Of even providence, of what grandfather sounded like when
He was watching wrestling or how my mother
Laughed when she was running after me
Under the clothes line in the backyard of
A house 65 years in the past now, a paradise
Key where the object of longing is missing
Like a deed or a lucky charm, it is the saudade
Of all we have, lost in fact, the stern dedication
Of a bridge in American, a statue in San Pedro,
Memorializing a Portuguese fisherman, our people
Carpenters, fishermen, dairy farmers, whalers,
Some worked in the mills or in the grey oblong
Factories where they manufactured golf balls,
Workers hand-wrapping string around tight wooden spheres
That they held in their hands as the machines
Whirled around them, with plastic coverings
Poured over a hardening shell, the object
Of a longing that might never return, saudade.

Winter Arrives in Mourning, Unaccompanied

As if still stood the test of time,
the dreams continue, in which
people who are no longer with
us, dance and visit and judge
you as if they never left. They
arrive, unaccompanied and fierce.
With no advance warning, you are
in the bathroom of a skyscraper, crying,
in front of a temp you never met,
shaking inside a shudder of the
cold you feel as if you will never be
able to turn away from, to do this
normal thing again or repeat one
word. It is not possible any more.
There was a border
and a finish line and the path
you were on has been rolled up
like a carpet in storage. And, still,
you stand there, holding a cardboard
box with a watch and a metal tray,
some yellow bits of paper and a jar
of hard cinnamon candy, tied around
the neck with a red ribbon. You think
of the escalator and being on it,
at Christmas, imagining
presents and the holiday. You get a coffee
as you used to do and say hello to Gayle.
Before things went south, you remember

looking down, and there are 50 stories
below. There is a special key you use
in the elevator and you stop before you get
off the floor where you used to work,
you kneel, to change your shoes so you
can take the stairs when the smoke
alarm goes off, as the first pink
spheres curl around your head
like a lullaby and you know in
an instant that this world ride
we are on will never be
the same.

Drinkers of Silence, Emigrants from Other Worlds

I sent you bracelets on your birthday,
and was surprised when you were sympathetic
after my mother died. You talked about surfing
and Long Beach, and it was strangely calming
when, during a time that I barely knew you,
and during a time when I was barely
getting by each day to wake up
from a dream that Audrey was still in the world,
and then getting slammed into a cement wall
when I remembered. Yeah. When I remembered.
The world was in a million pieces, none of
Them meant for me, you were on the phone.
It was a time for dancing only I wasn't.
There were terrorists and bombs
threatening America, and I was holding onto
a 6am job I could not pull myself to go to.
I remember showing up, in downtown
Los Angeles, off Figueroa. I was half a person,
a paper doll, with a sack full of cut out prom
dresses, and a box in which to put my office junk,
the Chevron coffee mug, a metal drawer
full of holiday decorations I used to care about.
The ski photo, posed in Utah when I had a purple
scarf. There was a special mouse pad
and my own blue stapler, labeled with my initials
so no one could steal it. Jumbo boxes of dry soup
and bubble gum. I went into the bathroom,
to change my shoes, as if it were a common day.

This Necessary World of Objects

Includes the ordinary
and the unnecessary,
I used to collect more things,
back when I used to know my
own mind, when I used to anticipate
my own needs about
what I wanted at the toss of
a quarter or dime, to decide
there was no sporting chance
because I used to know and
it was all right because it made
things, objects, like a prayer
events happened for me.
I was always collecting,
Spode china, silver
Drop earrings, creating a photogenic life.
Objects, clothes. A mural of what it looked
like to be me, to live as me.
I cannot believe now.
That I used to have a style,
I used to walk into a store and
Immediately recognize what jacket
was wanted and which shoes
(as I said often out loud) already belonged to me.

Far from the Honeyed-Wax Heart

from a line by PaulA Neves

Nobody knew if it was possible
when they first set out to try.
The soft weirdness of their
longing was but a knot in the
horizon of the harsh northern
path they were taking.
As if they had known all
along it would be so, this way,
the taking, like a newness they had
seen before
a trust. There was a beggar, stopping
in the middle
of communion and a virgin, fat
and common. The butchers they walked
past seemed endless, like a long city block.
If only their numbers paid off,
on each notch of the stick of hope
that the bringer of the horses had
told them about. Perhaps it would all
be revealed. Those who were once
believers, in the dark earth grow crafty
as butter when the journey continues
too long. Half-throwing down gauntlets
of sorrow, there are clouds overhead,
bats, coyotes, combat.
War is like this they said to each other before
they went back to sleep, as nervous

as the earth-born world they used to
know, now, shaky and green,
as the thoughts they used to have, of immortality,
of an aching, to reach wilderness, to drink in
the black water they called almost rain.
Almost rain, they can hear it in the rumbling
way off in the future-distant, just
like their freedom, it says, no.

More Nocturnal than the Sleep

It was more than a blackout,
a swift dullness, as if I were gonna
faint when my legs buckled under
neath me and my ears spun out
with fussy noise that grew louder
as the view in front of my eyes,
hollowed out and bleeding like water,
like ripples of water cascading
before my hands held out. It was not
sleep. It was more than lethargy, or
oblivion. It was more than a stupor
or me swooning over love.
It was an immediate force. A kick
in my bones, as thick as lumber.
I went down like a dislodged
boulder, in the middle of
the wall. Five tons dislodging
more than sleep, more than slumber
more than temporary.

The Only Answer to Silence

We talk to fill the wolf
and feed the billows above
gasping into lost breath
with a mouthful of air
held inside between coughs.
We listen to run the path
of the voices we follow,
and miss the seven bridges
home, past the blue afternoons
of scary left turns.
And, the yellow midnights
full of courage we cannot touch.
It seems oblivious to have these
symptoms
that take ahold inside, and yet
they are there, another year is over
and many life lessons later. The
only answer is to have none,
an allergy to distance and distract and pull
away as quickly as you can when
things get tight-fisted.

For Truth would be from a Line

inspired by Gastão Cruz

And, I would go, really.
And, is it about time we all got along,
but that was a no and the real answer would require
more sense than the crazy crisis
we are going through presently,
and the truth, ah. It would have to
be from a line
we used to know, an old phrase,
like a poem dealing with
trees I memorized, along with everyone
else in Mrs. Virtue's first grade
at Luther Burbank,
where the teacher handed out
pastel marshmallows
when we behaved.
For truth would have
to be untouchable,
like a hand we used to know,
to hold—
as if it were our own—
the left reaching
for the right, fumbling along thru
this magnificent universe we kind of
know, or at least pretended it to be so.

Unmade

for Carolina Matos

She couldn't put it away.
It was a night thought, an unfigured
out stratagem, she was inside of
the maze, the room where she was
locked inside for madness,
the place where she felt most
safe, as if she could no longer
harm anyone, and could relax,
insulting the wind that came
in under the locked door.
She screamed against the locked
door, white, its handle the color
of oyster shells, the floor, an uneven
tea stain, with its catty-corner
slats, diagonal from a right corner
nearest the window nailed shut.
She had wanted to be taken
here, when the house
they had shared was flooded,
boxes of family photos and the Portuguese
collector's stamps, catalogued
by movers, her husband's ghost
fading away, taken out with the gingham
wallpaper, peeled off in jagged splotches
away from the plaster wet walls
she was looking at.

Still not Ilha Enough

dedicated to Noel Quinones

Duty calling, obligations slip away
Like a drowning body into the water
Giving in and slipping away. The things we used
To count on, the appointments made
Are unbelievably easy to cancel
Like rolling off a log people used to say
There used to be such an importance
In how the house appeared the bathroom
Sink cleared of spots of dried toothpaste
And hair clinging to the sides of the basin
For dear life. A haircut, a job, how to pull
Over for gas at least once or twice a week,
The car now running down the battery over
Months of unused and dare I say it, neglect
The things we used to do willingly, the things
We were talked into as the right of form
Or passage now slip off our fingers like rings
In cold weather, gold rings slipping off
Fingers and disappearing into the frozen
like escaping through an open window.
Flights to the Azores are virtually empty
an oceanic archipelago in the mid North Atlantic
We whisper the word archipelago
If measured from their base at the very
bottom of the ocean, to their peaks,
the islands are among the tallest mountains.

And, at last, God Returns

Sordid and sallow, a harsh
disappointment
to the prepared flock awaiting
for salvation or the next thing
coming, the judgement call
or all judgement calls.
The reckoning or the vanishing.
The end of the narrative.
What is it they call it? The
Rapture, and not in a sexual
way, when the faithful are
suddenly taken above, under
the dove wing of god, leaving
behind only the sinners, the
men and women who walk
the blind earth, able-bodied
and kind, perhaps they do not
know or are yet to have lived their
delicious lives, yet un-indoctrinated
into the secret work of Christ or
deliverance of hatred. The
salvation, a sweetness alone,
like a small boy
who cannot find the last puzzle
piece to the lake with the swans
on the family table and is punished for it.

I've Driven all Night through a Grainy Landscape

All the answers, I used to know,
repeated again and again, as if they were
lines in a political game, trying to talk
someone into believing, as they say
in apples and a banana and then go forth
into a world where there are walls
built across artificial boundaries,
and families torn apart inside the parallel
lines of truth. It is what it is and that
means even if it kills me, I will be true
to my own patience. It's agonizing, I know,
every single time, the visits are painful,
the release is impossible to recreate.
It's a total body experience, granted
and guaranteed to take me somewhere I can
smile and normalize things as they should
be, as I recalled them—just not yesterday.
But, last year, it didn't take weeks
for the clock to click one minute to
three like when you were a kid, agonizing
to go home. And then there are the waiters,
not food service but those who are patient,
for diagnosis, for tests, for death.
The mid-line boundary between
someone saying everything is gonna be
OK and everything is over. It is the passage
Of that long journey, that I have
to work myself up to face, to make it

Through borders and boundaries, week after
week for the past year, a life lived,
sawed in half like a magic trick. I am
perched on the edge of, ready to
nod or run. Waiting makes you swear
someone was loved and kind once, and
that to make it all OK again, there is
wishing, a hope for it to be as it was,
when it was perceived to be all right
but perhaps it never was. And, so,
to normalize interactions, the daily hellos
we take for granted, the guarantees we
make with each other must be labeled
seared into agreements that we promise
to be civil or polite to each other, the nods
at the bus stop, basic remnants of life
in front of a modicum of human happiness.
But my heart also breaks. In truth, it hurts a lot
Because the heart knows what my
job is. The hurt is the pain above
it all, the others keep moving away, to form
new shapes, now, and when I want them
to stay close, they stick to me like glue.
Longing is the middle ground, when you have
distant connections. It's such a hard place to be in.
The waiting and the hoping for a time
When you won't wait any longer then, feeling lived,
a life guilty for that thought. Then, it all runs together
in time, like dirty rivers, seeking a new mouth.

Endnotes

The poems in *Through a Grainy Landscape* were primarily influenced and inspired by the following work from Portuguese-American writers and Portuguese writers in translation: "Poems from the Portuguese" (www.poemsfromtheportuguese.org), a comprehensive anthology of 21st century Portuguese poetry, conceived by Ana Hudson, sponsored by Centro Nacional De Cultura. Specific works are noted below.

Thank you for the wisdom and insight.

Lines, titles and quotes

"The body is a distant lost city" by João Miguel Fernandes Jorge

"This Love is Not Made of Blood" inspired by the poem, "I abandon you each night …" by Armando Silva Carvalho

"No Train will Take us This Far" inspired by the poem, "A Parallel Life' by Rui Pires Cabral

"That Much is Obvious" from a line by Brian Sousa, in "Praça do Comercio"

"Resentful Women" by Margarida Vale de Gato

"I've Driven all Night through a Grainy Landscape," a revisiting of "I've driven all night through a grainy landscape" by Tiago Araújo

"To you Who saw Fjords and Corals," was inspired by a quote from Renata Correia Botelho

"A Man sleeps, the Skies Move" inspired by "XXVI," a poem by Luis Quintais

"Where your Mouth Delays the Cut" is inspired by Marques Gastão's poem "Be Firewood"

"An Unsuitable Green" is inspired by a poem by Yvette K. Centeno called "Through the Looking Glass"

"Drinkers of Silence, from the poem "Lisbon," by Diogo Vaz Pinto

"This Necessary World of Objects" is inspired by the poem "Wallace Stevens on his Way to the Office" by Pedro Mexi

"One never returns to the same place" is a line by Isabel Aguiar

"Carrying Someone You'd not Seen in 15 Years" was inspired by, "1963: The Lord Giveth," a poem by Sam Pereira

"All Open to the Heat" comes from a line in the poem "City in Summer" by Gastão Cruz

"Winter Arrives in Mourning, Unaccompanied" stems from a poem by Sérgio Godinho, "Night is Day"

"Far from the Honeyed-Wax Heart" is from a poem entitled, "Offerings Ofensas" by PaulA Neves

Indirect influences

a line in the story "Fado" by Katherine Vaz

Golgona Anghel's poem, "In insomnia's reading room"

a poem called "A Book by Dylan Thomas" by Manuel de Freitas

a poem called, "women are the ones who" by Bénédicte Houart

a poem called "Fresh bread" by João Luís Barreto Guimarães

a poem called "Marthiya of Abdel Hamid according to Alberto Pimenta 4" by Alberto Pimenta

Grateful thanks to the Luso writers the author reviewed and/or interviewed: Sam Pereira, Nuno Júdice, Frank Gaspar, Rosa Alice Branca, Donna Freitas, Carlo Matos, Anthony de Sa, Brian Sousa, Amy Sayre Baptista, PaulA Neves, Stephen Rebello, José Luís Peixoto, Darrell Kastin, Alberto Pimento, Irene Marques, Nancy Vieira Couto, Katherine Vaz, Vamberto Freitas, George Monteiro, Alice Clemente, Anthony Barcelos, Marina Carreira, Lara Gularte, Diniz Borges, Elaine Ávila, Hugo dos Santos, Deolinda Adão, Jacinto Lucas Pires and others. And, with much appreciation to *The Portuguese American Journal* (where many of these interviews first appeared).

Acknowledgments

GRATEFUL ACKNOWLEDGMENT is extended to the following publications in which these poems (or previous versions) first appeared:

Anomaly: "Carrying Someone You'd not Seen in 15 years"
Another Chicago Magazine: "I Abandon you Each Night"
Bookends Review: "More Nocturnal than the Sleep"
Bosphorus Review (Turkey): "So Much Needs to be Said"
Blue Collar Review: "Broken Bottles and Rivers"
Broadkill Review: "And Rage — a Pot of Orchids you Loved"
Elephants Never: "Because this One is Broken," and "An Unsuitable Green"
FlowerSong Press: Good Cop/Bad Cop: An Anthology: "Nothing Inside you but the Wool of your Sorrows"
California Quarterly: "Rust Imposed" and "Mother wearing glasses and a scarf"
Gavea-Brown: "Mixing Drinks," "I Smoke my Dead Cigarette in too Much Haste," "Where your Mouth Delays the Cut," "And There was Red Fish," "With Myself I Disagree"
Globalpoemic: "The Undoing" "For Truth would be from a Line"
The Journal: "A Man Sleeps, The Skies Move"
Laurel Review: "I've Driven all Night through a Grainy Landscape." "A Representation of Itself"
Mantis: "The Most Vertical of Words"
New American Writing: "Unmade" and "The Only Answer to Silence"
Poetry Salzburg Review: "It Was My Mother Who Taught Me to Fear"
Poets and Artists: "Woman in a YelloX Dress"
Portuguese Literary & Cultural Studies 31 (UMAss): "With Eyes that Bear the Widowhood of Days," "The Graphics of Home," and, "At Last, God Returns."
Quiddity: "This Necessary World of Objects"
Queen Mob's Teahouse: "When Are You Going to Berlin"
The Santa Barbara Literary Journal: "Of a Verbal Silence," and "To you, Who Saw Fjords and Coral"
Tinfish: "I Ask You Not to Leave Tomorrow"

Special Acknowledgments

THANKS TO the National Endowment for the Arts, the California Arts Council; CantoMundo; Fulbright, FLAD (Luso-American Foundation in Portugal); the Corporation of Yaddo; Jentel; Fundación Valparaíso in Mojacar, Spain; Foundation for Contemporary Arts (NYC), and Barbara Deming Foundation (Money for Women) for their generous support and encouragement. Through a Grainy Landscape was a Finalist in the New Rivers, Many Voices Project, and at Trio House Press. Special thanks to FACA, Westside Women Writers, Luis Gonçalves and Kale Soup for the Soul. And, as always, with gratefulness, to Charles.

NEA fellow, Millicent Borges Accardi, a Portuguese-American writer, is the author of three poetry collections. She holds degrees in English and literature from California State University, Long Beach and the University of Southern California. Among her awards are fellowships from the National Endowment for the Arts, California Arts Council, Fulbright, CantoMundo, Creative Capacity, Foundation for Contemporary Arts NYC (COVID grant), Yaddo, Fundação Luso-Americana (Portugal), and Barbara Deming Foundation. Her poems have appeared in *New Letters*, *Laurel Review*, *Tampa Review* and *Nimrod*. Millicent lives in Topanga, California.

Made in United States
North Haven, CT
12 July 2023